Pagan Poems
Volume I

Carolyn Emerick

Contents

Liminal Places	5
Visions in the Night	7
The Moonlit Path	9
In Der Schwartzwald	11
The Mystic Misty Moon	15
Spirits of Samhain	17
Lightening's Strike	19
Well of Wonder	23
The Warrior's Passage	25
The Cold Winter Night	29
The Song of the Wind	33
Silvery Light on Samhain Night	35
Sonnet to Starlight	37
The Enchanted Stream	38
Vagabond	41
Vampire Moon	43
Under Cloudy Scottish Skies	45
A Dream Within A Dream	47
Azure Sky	49
Rhythmic Forces	51
The Faerie Dance	53

The Mystic Wood by John William Waterhouse

Liminal Places

Liminal places and moonlit faces,
dewdrops upon my skin.
Stardust traces and soft embraces,
a magical journey begins

Guided by voices, not by my choices
an ethereal pathway appears.
Following noises and Fae Folk rejoices,
their music drifts into my ears.

From behind a tree, looking at me
are antlers and two glowing eyes.
Can it be? It could only be he.
The Horned One, his shadow belies.

He made not a sound while he carried me down
to the bank by the side of the stream.
There on the ground, I thought I would drown
by passions awakened inside me.

Fille Au Citronnier by Émile Vernon

Visions in the Night

Dare to gaze in someone's eyes
behold the soul within.
For deep inside the mind there lies
magic; waiting to begin.

Unlock the door that hides the soul
let the spirit free.
Imagination takes control,
a different realm we see.

Cast a spell of slumber
and begin to dream a dream.
Awaken to discover
it's more real than it can seem.

Illustration by Emma Florence

The Moonlit Path

Standing on the precipice,
do I take the leap?
Shall I start the journey
to discover what I seek?

Behold, the stars they beckon,
and I can hear the calls
of magic laden voices
who whisper I must fall.

Upon this very precipice,
today I must decide.
Do I heed the calling?
Or is it just my pride?

Will the starlight guide me
to my journey's end?
Is the magic real enough,
or is it just pretend?

This precipice of indecision
a prison may become.
There is moonlight on the path ahead,
and so I sojourn on.

Illustration by Arthur Rackham

In Der Schwartzwald

Schwartzwald, Schwartzwald,
dark and dense.
So many tales
have been told hence.

Wolves and princess,
dwarves and prince.
They make us laugh
and sometimes wince.

Schwartzwald with such
dark green trees.
Stay on the path
and you may meet

The Lady who will
bless your fate.
Stay the course,
don't deviate.

Illustration by H. J. Ford

For off the path,
if you be pulled,
an evil one
dressed in wool

may tempt you with
an apple sweet.
Please don't bite it,
don't you eat!

But, if an ugly
croaking frog
should like to give
a little snog,

if you are too
proud to kiss,
your soulmate's love
you may have missed!

O, Schwartzwald does
it's treasures give.
In my Elfin heart
may always live.

Felsküste im Mondschein by Johann Nomuk Schödlberger

The Mystic Misty Moon

The mystic misty moon,
and so he glows, so he glows.
A phosphorescent crescent,
how he smiles, for he knows.

The nighttime air is damp
after freshly fallen rain.
Your moist breath upon my skin
would almost feel the same.

The misty glowing moonlight,
how he shines, how he shines.
As he's gazing down upon me,
he seems to read my mind

O' golden orb against dark skies,
a velvet bed of blue.
If I could ask him for one wish,
then I would ask for you.

Spirits of Samhain

Without words the Old Ways call
to their children far and wide.
Return home, they beckon us
to the spirits left behind.

In the dead of night I hear a voice
though there is no sound.
A ghostly wind that carries me
to the Sidhe's own mound.

Embers, embers burning bright,
call forth the spirits of this night!
Rising from their gloomy graves,
chant the spells writ on the staves.

Samhain Eve'n conjures up
souls who have departed.
And the wicked women know
what witchcraft has just started.

Siegmund & Sieglind by Mariano Fortuny

Lightening's Strike

Curled up tight in my cocoon
because I could not face the day,
someone whom I love so much
was about to slip away.

So many challenges I've overcome,
but this, I could not face.
For the one who always held me close
to vanish without a trace.

But, love transcends the mortal realm,
and this I now do know.
A new love was sent my way,
the greatest gift bestowed.

Springtime by Pierre Auguste Cot

The spirits of my ancestors
a plan they did contrive.
Stardust sprinkled on our souls
and the stars they did align.

The one who makes me feel complete
has come into my life
Love has struck like lightening,
and zapped away all strife.

Once I lived in darkness,
but now I'm shining like the sun.
For when two flames are joined together,
they join and burn as one.

Illustration by Rie Cramer

Well of Wonder

Gazing in the well of wonder,
it is your face I see?
Scrying, I am trying to discover
if you are looking back at me.

The gods have gazed inside this well,
but their talent I have not.
Transfixed am I, under your spell.
My heart and mind in knots.

The universe this well does hold,
yet, my vision it is clear.
When the world will shift and fold,
I promise I'll be near.

Through this tunnel of time and space,
are you looking at the moon?
Look closely, can you see my face?
Or will this end too soon?

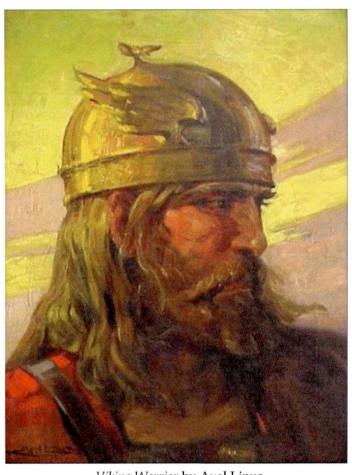

Viking Warrior by Axel Linus

The Warrior's Passage

Peering through the portal
into the other realms,
a wanderer seeking passage
must first don the helm.

A helm of fortitude and courage,
and aching thirst for the truth.
Then let go and place thy faith in
the sweet dark sayer of sooth.

With cold and steely gaze
she will look behind thine eyes.
Thy words are only edifice,
true character the soul belies.

If the wanderer is worthy,
she will cast the runes.
To whither thou art heading,
the journey beginneth soon.

The Norns by Alois Delug

While this Wicce may be cunning,
alone she doth not work.
She enters trance and calls upon
the Norns who weave thy Wyrd.

Past, present and future
are written on thy web.
Thy place in life is woven tight,
but soon that tide will ebb.

She handeth thee a gemstone
etched with the Helm of Awe.
"Hold this sigil betwixt thy brow
and thy foe shall turn to straw!"

A wanderer thou beganeth,
a warrior shalt thou become.
When thy weaponry and spirit
shall merge and fight as one.

Photo by Carolyn Emerick

The Cold Winter Night

I long for him to kiss me
in the cold, cold winter wind.
The wider world starts spinning
leaving only me and him.

His eyes, they penetrate me
while his hands clutch my hips.
His rough beard upon my skin,
and the soft heat in his lips.

From far away I saw his face
which touched me deep inside.
But it wasn't only physical,
it was the measure of his mind.

By Tom Lovell

He stands with firm convictions,
and is true to what is right.
Though there is such darkness,
he sees the beauty and the light.

When the winter wind is howling,
in the night it's all I hear.
I think of him so far away
and wish that he were near.

His arms wrapped around me,
body pressed against mine tight.
His hot breath upon my skin
in this cold, cold winter night.

Photo by Carolyn Emerick

The Song of the Wind

Lay me down in the green, green moss,
a fallen tree to rest my head.
The soft natural ground,
with the leaves fallen down
is all I need to make my bed.

Sing me to sleep with the song of the wind,
its fingers caress my skin.
The birds of the morn
will herald the dawn,
and another new journey begins.

Mermaids by Konstantin Yegorovich Makovsky

Silvery Light on Samhain Night

Forswear I saw by the light of the moon,
 those I've loved had gone too soon.
And silvery light betrayed my sight.
True beauty, I knew thee not tonight!

Those who know, we cannot teach
Earth's rhythmic patterns whom to reach.
 'Tis a grace innate to some,
 whilst others live in aberration.

Disconnected from the ebb and flow,
they live unconscious, whilst yet *we* know.
Tides like breath heave out and in.
Moon phases change, as doth the wind.

Crackling static energy fields,
 most are immune, but some do feel.
Messages pour through the other side.
Try as we might, we cannot hide.

Yet, by the silvery light of this moon,
 in a dream or in a swoon,
what I have known, or could so well,
that which I know, I cannot tell.

Aurora and Cephalus by Baron Pierre Narcisse Guerin

Sonnet to Starlight

Only in the blackest night
the stars' bright light is seen.
Though I tried with all my might
to see them in my dreams.
Sleeping, though I'm wide awake,
my vision it was blurred.
If my heart you were to take,
would your own be stirred?
In the blackest dead of night
I feel you close beside.
Your presence takes away my fright,
I no longer need to hide.
In starlight does your spirit glow,
it is the soul I've known of old.

Photo by Carolyn Emerick

The Enchanted Stream

And when ye wake inside a dream,
seek ye the enchanted stream.
For those who have the will to look
may find the guardian of the brook.

And if thine heart be fair and true
as reflections in the morning dew,
if thine courage be not meek,
so shall ye find the one ye seek.

For if thou keep a magical mind,
without searching, so shall ye find
treasures not of Earthly birth,
formed by the measure of thy worth.

And if fair maiden thine heart desires,
the one who lights thy soul afire,
ye need not fear, ye need not weep,
for thou art destined one day to meet.

Thine stars have surely cast their lots
for a love born of Camelot.
So if ye wake inside thine dream,
thy visions be more real than seemed.

The Kiss of the Siron by Gustav Wertheimer

Vagabond

Perambulating through this life,
a vagabond I have been.
The future had been undetermined,
free to every whim.

Lovers, they have come and gone,
and I've possessed a few.
But none have truly held my heart
in a way that's true

And then I gazed upon a face
whose soul peered back at me.
He touched me somewhere deep inside,
and set my passions free.

It's an irrational attraction,
an all-consuming flame.
A thunderbolt has surely struck,
and I will never be the same.

The Lone Wolf by Alfred Wierusz-Kowalski

Vampire Moon

Ethereal light and tranquility
shining down with this full moon.
Clear skies transmit so much energy,
this night can but end all too soon.

My skin must hide from the hot summer sun,
and shirk from the brightness of day.
It's when the glory of night has begun,
my fears, they do start to dissuade.

The others, they seem to thrive in the day.
But, I live for the darkness of night.
That's when my creatures come out to play,
but the daylight, it's shine makes us hide.

A shining disc of custard lights up my way.
My gods, such ambience is rare.
If you meet my wolf as we're out here to play,
then you better be braced for a scare.

Scottish Highlands by Gustave

Under Cloudy Scottish Skies

Take me in the Scottish countryside
in the green rolling hills.
Take possession of my body,
and bend me to your will.

Lay me down in soft green grass,
kiss me roughly on my lips.
I ache to feel your body weight
pressing down upon my hips.

Hold down my arms above my head
and look deep into my eyes.
My body is your's, so take me there
under cloudy Scottish skies.

The Vision of Endymion by Edward John Poynter

A Dream Within a Dream

To fall asleep with in your mind
thoughts of one so fair and kind;
subconsciously doth the mind unfold
to glimpse a place as yet untold.

To dream a dream within a dream,
so magical that it may seem
between reality and fantasy.

The moon beaming brightly down
we gracefully float above the ground.
Reach to touch the shining stars...
Will stardust erase previous scars?

To dream a dream of ecstasy,
I close my eyes and start to scream
can I make my dream reality?

The New Moon by Albert Aublet

Azure Sky

Oh to be with the one whom I love
under fantastical evening skies.
Glory of angels with grace like the doves,
such a sky that I saw here tonight

The sun still brilliant, blazing itself low,
azure canvas awaits its first kiss.
Passionfruit streaks sucking red glow
upon the virgin's blue skin.

Beauty, majesty, knowledge of things
deeper than most comprehend.
When my eyes behold such deep truth,
then I know that I'm yours 'til the end.

Miranda by Frederick Goodall

Rhythmic Forces

Rhythmic fluctuations flow
like palpitations, so they go.
Earth energies, a static zing
amplified by heart's beating.

A conduit for fluid force,
as raging rivers chart their course.
Overwhelming electric power
that keeps increasing by the hour.

If these sensations one can feel,
they be governed by what is real.
Learn to channel what is true,
lest your senses rule you.

Nymphs Dancing to Pan's Flute by Joseph Tomanek

The Faerie Dance

A bluebell awakes me from my sleep,
gently toward the sound I creep.
I scarcely can believe my eyes
scores of golden fireflies!

The moon beams his magic down,
stardust sprinkled on the ground.
A pixie dancing in the glen;
a sight I'll never see again.

Stardust shines upon the leaves,
such beauty cannot be believed.
Sprites giggle with delight,
and mischievously play throughout the night.

But, only 'til the break of Dawn
this ballet of magic can dance on.
When up is the Sun with his first ray of light,
the faerie creatures flit out of sight -
to await the blue mystique of night.

About the Author

Carolyn Emerick generally writes about European folk tradition. She is also an avid lover of literature and poetry. Carolyn holds a bachelor's degree in literature and is pursuing a master's degree in English.

Read more at www.CarolynEmerick.com,

and follow on Facebook at:

www.Facebook.com/CarolynEmerick.Writer.

Made in the USA
Middletown, DE
29 November 2020